CRACKS

YOU

OPEN

CRACKS YOU OPEN

poetry & musings

RENEE PEDIGO

On Again Press

For the fellow broken hearts.

CONTENTS

INTRODUCTION

FALLING

falling	3
tumbling	4
your heart	6

STAYING

into my world	13
crazy bird	14
relationship fantasy	15

LOSING

will you win this one?	19
my shattered door	20
questioning myself	23
knee doctor reports	25
the other side	27

LEAVING

i'm so tired   31

i bought you a present   32

i forgive you for me   34

the past of us   35

easy does it   37

one of those nights   39

the plants died   41

i'll see you   42

happy holidays   44

lucky reality   47

still awake   50

where were we?   51

this still comes to me, even after it all   54

you'll always be the one   55

torn and wrinkled   58

whole hole   60

what is it?   64

my cat pee   66

my lonely company   69

shriveled broken bits   73

your greatest gift   75

LOVING AGAIN

secret beach   81

what's left for what's next   83

hey stranger hey   86

boar's head   88

love is   90

in hopes with hope   93

tie-dye girl   96

MANTRAS

ACKNOWLDEGMENTS

RESOURCES

INTRODUCTION

This selection of poems and musings follows my journey with love—falling, staying, losing, leaving, and loving again. It has not been a linear path, nor has it been isolated. The living, processing, and unraveling I have experienced—and that has found me—is interwoven with every other part of my being. My family's generational trauma and my complex post-traumatic stress disorder are embedded in each word. The stark reality of confronting my difficult coping mechanisms, seeing them clearly, holding them, and enduring the uncomfortable stages of releasing them saturates each stanza. The process of opening myself to new ways of living is woven into each line.

These pages hold my reflections as I've moved through this season of life's defining moments. It is a snapshot of how my first love has shaped me—both in its presence and absence.

I invite you to sit with the emotions that arise as you move through these pages. There is no rush. There are no expectations. There is no need to finish.

I hope these words offer support on your healing journey. You are not alone. Take it slow and keep moving forward. You are exactly where you need to be right now. I hope you write down what you need, when you need it, at every point along the way.

Love is beautiful
difficult
enriching
exhausting
and all
worth it

Love you
over
again & again,

Renee

This book contains content that might be troubling for some readers, including, but not limited to themes of generational trauma, suicide, mental illness, and complex post-traumatic stress disorder.

Please be mindful of these and other possible triggers and seek assistance if needed from resources on page 107.

FALLING

FALLING

falling four weeks in
but when seconds feel like days
hours feel like months
four weeks in, you know

> I say I'm falling
> but I'm here
> you say you thought
> and you know too

crazy
wild
is this really happening?

> enjoy
> breathe
> be here
> be with me

it's easy, that's when
comfort is unconscious, that's how
open in love, that's why

> this is

here

> now

you

> us

           partner

TUMBLING

everyone says 30 is when you come into yourself
30 is when the lights turn on
30 is when you shed those final flakes of living for
anyone else but yourself
caring deeply for anyone else's thoughts but your own

30 is
loving yourself so immensely
you stand a little taller
fill out your life a little smoother
move like the wind,
without question,
a natural progression and flow of energy

I feel this energy peeking its head into my life

from the release of people
who treat me less than I deserve
from sitting in my uncomfortable patterns
and exposing them to the sunlight

by forgiving myself for the doubt, fear, and shame
I've felt for being human
perfectly imperfect

it's not quite made its way fully in
it's not quite smooth
the rocks of my subconscious are still tumbling
fear still holds its grip on my throat from time to time

I get shy
I feel more

scream more
cry more

I feel the pain
of shedding those habits I used to cling to for dear life
in the hopes that if I held on tight enough
then maybe I would be enough

but I've let go
I've released the grip
falling, flailing
there is no known destination
only the intention to be free

more fully myself
no matter the room
more of whatever I'm feeling at that moment
no matter the "vibes" of the group

more colorful
more whole
more of me
more free

this is 29
still tumbling
with hope to shine

YOUR HEART

you're the only thing on my mind
from the morning through the night
when I wake to leave
you're still fast asleep
I hold you tight

I kiss the crevice between your chin
in that moment you cuddle up to my heart
silent and strong
I love you more and more as life goes on

it doesn't matter
your gender, your sex, your pedigree
it doesn't matter
your race, your complexion, your destiny
no, my love, that doesn't matter to me

it's your tenderness, your energy, your heart
it's your soul, your kindness, your spark
it's our connection from the start
it's you, my love, that matters to me

sometimes I beat myself up for it being different
than I imagined it would be
for it not being a part of my
canvas of a manipulated memory

sometimes has become less and less

cause I started living in my body instead of my head

you've taught me that you see

you've helped me with my longing
you've shown me there are other ways to live a life
you've taught me to calm down, take a breath and
how to relieve my own strife

you've taught me it's okay to fall down and let go
it's okay to collapse into someone
you're still getting to know
it's okay you don't know what's going to happen next
in fact, the key is you'll never
"get it," "figure it out," or digress

getting it is what I used to hold onto, cling to at night
it used to be the sun in my universe, the light
I used to laser-point my focus on just that
I used to say it will all be okay,
just get there so this can be your past

but now my love
holy shit babe
you've opened my world
there's light in my cave

I see more in the crevices of my life
I appreciate them and want to lick them
and celebrate their cries
I see the little scratches and scars as something
completely different than before
I look around and I see my open doors

I see lovingness, compassion, community
I see suffering couples with vulnerability
I see a range of life, of time, of choice
I see what it means to finally feel my true voice

I see this all from what I see in you
I see this more every day in a new view
I see so much in that kiss in the morning light
when my third eye is all on you
and your eyes are still shut tight

in that moment right before
anything else has a chance to start
in that moment
I feel your heart

STAYING

INTO MY WORLD

today I decided to get lost on the internet
in my book, this new show
leave this physical realm and dive deeper into
a new world, one I don't know

one where everyone believes in me
my moments of doubt are brief
brief enough to motivate me and build
but after that, I'm always granted relief

I lay on the ground next to the couch
because it feels better on my back
and because a new location felt like a good excuse
for continuing my meditation nap

it was neither and both

the closest I can get to stepping outside
is opening my back door
and feeling the brisk cold air
no more

the barrier of the screen door still intact
a couple seconds, back inside
where I don't lack

deeper into my world

CRAZY BIRD

I got something

                I don't know what it is

      but it's undiagnosed

it's just that

              I feel like a bird sometimes
                    pecking along
         eating my little seeds on the ground

      and alllllll of a sudden

another bird comes swooping in
trying to eat my seeds

            and I'm like woahhhhhhh
                the fuck
              looking around
        is anyone else seeing this

          but I'm also trying to eat my seeds
and I'm caught in this dual dilemma
          but I'm also still eating the seeds

so from the outside

                I look crazy

but from the inside

                I am crazy

      so you see my problem?

RELATIONSHIP FANTASY

it's hard not to get caught up in a fantasy
especially after the honeymoon phase ends

like I have this one
where my partner and I are lying in bed together
it's the morning
we're tossing and turning
and we both get up together
at the
same
time

that's it
that's the fantasy

see we work completely different schedules
and neither of our schedules are consistent
I'm a comedian trying to make it
and he's a singer

my fantasy is to have a consistent schedule
god that would make me come instantly

he's always like what turns you on
I'm like a 401K
Roth IRA
specifically
maybe just some consistency

WILL YOU WIN THIS ONE?

it's the quiet wars
that are the hardest

MY SHATTERED DOOR

it's funny how my past me
became my present me so fast
it's funny how I'm a comedian
but my specialty is sadness

I'm sitting here wondering
what comes next
thinking if I'm going to survive
this treacherous path

cause I don't know how to live anymore
trying to figure out how to choose myself
instead of drowning out at the shore

but what I need is not from you
and what I am is so confused

you told me you could but you didn't
and I picked up the pieces anyway
your promises beautiful, eloquent
but insane to think
anything would be different than before
and all I'm left with is a shattered door

last night I read you the poem that changed me
last night I was transported to another life fictitiously

I want to believe in the fairy tale
of change
I want to feel that ecstasy
instead of the pain

but a mirage evaporates eventually
and if it doesn't
it turns out you're living in insanity

and what I need is the impeccable truth
and what I am is bruised

you told me you could but you didn't
and I picked up the pieces anyway
your promises beautiful, eloquent
am I insane to think
that anything would be different than before?
and all I'm left with is a shattered door

raw and revealing
punctured but healing
the doorknobs loose
but I can still turn the key

I ask myself if I can trust this
or if I trust this
am I turning on the one person who needs me most?
am I stunting my own growth?

you told me you could but you didn't
and I picked up the pieces anyway
your promises beautiful, eloquent
and I don't need to listen anymore

I found out

I have
other doors

and now all I need
is to
leave

this shattered door

QUESTIONING MYSELF

I keep questioning this thing
guess it's not quite guaranteed

                what does that mean?
                  what does it mean?

if we can't be what we need
if we don't quite feel free

                what does that mean?
                  what does it mean?

I've been trying and trying and trying and trying
and trying and trying and trying and trying
but we're here again

                does that make sense?

you asked me
to dive in deep
to see what I mean when I mean
I don't know how
this scares me

I know it's never going to be
always easy

but how do I know
if it's not easy for now
or if it will never be easy to make that vow

I can't help feeling this is more than a storm
cause the small things keep building
and I don't know where this goes

what does that mean?
what does it mean?

I want to talk to say
I can't keep living this way
I feel I've tried to show
and I don't want to let you go
but this feeling keeps growing
it's not feeling okay

and if okay is the goal
I don't know if I want this anymore

cause I keep questioning myself

I'm confused as hell

I don't want to be afraid
but I don't know if I want to stay

KNEE DOCTOR REPORTS

my knees may never recover
from standing on them for two years

I forgot what it felt like to be on two feet
happy and healthy
walking with your partner

I dragged pounds of promises on broken scabs
freshly bleeding as quickly as it pretended to heal
you can't heal hopes that are still being ripped open
by ever-empty words you let ooze out

what's worse?
a phantom never present
or a puppet never used

my dream of reality was shaded in bright prospects
obsessed with the potential
while disregarding the weight of inaction

choosing to believe that one day
you'll mean it
what you say

that day finally came
for someone else

you gave someone new
the beginning of their next heartbreak
I hope she has stronger ankles than me

the doctor says the cartilage in my knees

will never recover
the only hope is for the muscles

so they give me small cures for current times only
promising no hope
or false visions
or lies

it's refreshing to have a taste of respect

like the bitter bite of a fresh slice of lime
poignant, pungent but pure every time

THE OTHER SIDE

does my new house haunt you
like our old home haunts me?

do you feel my presence
when you drink your coffee?

cause I feel you every day still
and I wonder what lies there

on the other side of
this string of us

.

LEAVING

I'M SO TIRED

I'm so tired of trying to be a
good daughter
good friend
good lover
good girl
good woman

I'm so tired of trying

I don't want to try to be any more
I just want to be
then try

try what I want
while I just be

that's what I want
that's what I will be
that's what's next for me

I BOUGHT YOU A PRESENT

I'm sad I didn't feel more grateful then
I'm guilty that I couldn't have just said Thank You
and played pretend
I'm kicking myself as I wear the slippers here
I relive the moment you gave them to me
in every tear

I see your reaction
the love, the joy, the ecstasy
I remember I gave you that

while you gave me a guilty moment in time

I think about that trip
and wonder why we did it
then remember all the times
we did it for you

I fall deeper and deeper into my guilt
of not appreciating what I had
but not sticking up for what I deserved more of
I didn't feel special and I know why
and I don't need to feel guilty inside

you didn't not show up because of me
you didn't show up because of you
it's your baggage you carried and I took it on too

I said it's okay, I said next time then
but next time came and I was left sitting there
wondering what I did to deserve this

to not be thought of
to not be considered
to wither away and give so much
then be left in slivers

I have splinters from how many nights I spent
working on something special for you
my checking account deficiency is nothing compared
to my energy bank of point zero zero zero two

you sat there thinking of you
I sat there thinking of you
now I'm stuck here thinking of you
and of how much I thought too much of you

how much I gave you and what I've lost
how neither of us could give the other what we
wanted

how much did it all cost?

I FORGIVE YOU
FOR ME

flashes of our community
we build it from scratch

scratch that
we grew it from nothing

but nothing can go back to nothing
as fast as the spring flowers die
doesn't matter how often you water them
a cycle is a cycle that ends

I thought I was waiting for your apologies
but I needed oxygen sooner than that

so I forgive you for me

I see all the joy that was
the parts I miss
flashes of the scratches rouse the anger

so I step forward for me

the bruises will heal
the past will fade
I'll be there
at my next atmospheric shift
with a new catalyst

there I will remember

I forgave you for me

THE PAST OF US

I'm oozing out the past of us
I feel the puss alive on my skin
I want to know when I'll stop thinking of you
or if this is just how it is

I woke up crying
from a dream we were in
we were just laughing
and taking photos to begin

Three miles in and my feet keep moving
cause it makes it a little easier to face the day
I can't take this meeting or be in this space
not when I don't know if I'm okay

I want you still
I want you here now
and that breaks my heart more

cause I don't know how you feel
and I'm supposed to not think about it, sure

I wish we wanted the same things
I wish we could have grown together

I wish that I could hold you
no matter the past
no matter the weather

I cry out harder when I realize
that's all we have anymore
all that's left of us

will be the past

no more laughing about our fart scents
no more date day presents

no more working towards something with you
no more ramen for two

now it's just me
with your memory
and I don't know where you are

now it's just my growth, my goals
and then you
somewhere
in your car

now I'll try to release
I'll try to let go
but just know

I'll hold the past of you present as I flow

EASY DOES IT

any specials today?
it's strange seeing you everywhere
but not seeing you anymore

I can feel you next to me now
but I know it's a dub

I'm substituting you
like a topping on my breakfast sandwich

easy over, easy does it
I'm too fragile to eat this early

the cats scratch at the back of my neck
pain lives here as a friend
they hiss more than they used to
and I leak more on cue

visions flood my vision
I'm trying to drown myself in love
so at least my lack of oxygen
has a decent sub

I go through a dozen much slower
I feel more gentle
I still want you, still dream of us
still see our kids playing in a rush

a rush to live more
a rush to discover
a rush to dive deeper
I need to recover

I don't know how to look
and not see you inside

I don't know how to walk
and not crumble every time

I don't know how to love
and not consider your smile

I don't know how to let go
even just for a while

the cat keeps bringing me her favorite feather
and I'm too weak to pick it up
I envy it forever

I wish I could feel its peace
I wish I could be its ease
I wish it could be me
I wish I was free

I'll have sausage and butter
no eggs

easy does it

ONE OF THOSE NIGHTS

sometimes I wonder
if you're eating potstickers for dinner too

cause tonight's just one of those nights

I didn't have soy sauce
so I made something up

                                    you sent me
                        all the money you owed me
                                    unexpectedly
I cried

I wish I could talk to you
wish I knew what was going on

                                    in your life

I'm like a burnt crispt outside
still frozen innards
a potsticker barely edible

            it's just one of those nights

I'm thinking of reaching out and saying Thank You
how easy it would be

I wonder if I called you out of the blue
if you'd pick up
and we'd talk for hours
like we used to

but I don't

I eat my dumplings instead
and hope somewhere in this city

you're doing the same
in your bed

THE PLANTS DIED

I dreamed you died last night
and I wasn't invited to the funeral
I woke up in tears at five a.m.
I thought of calling you right away
but cuddled myself back to sleep instead

I still love you
I still want to love you more
I'm still thinking of ways to surprise you and help
build our lives stronger, sturdier, grounded

some of the plants died since I left
but not the one your mother gave me
it's grown two new leaves
which makes me even more sad I had to leave

days like this make it hard to remember why this was
the "right" thing
my mood stays steady
like the overcast weather report
sprinkled showers
all-day

I'LL SEE YOU

I know I'll never run into you in the mornings
cause mornings have never been your thing

I know I'll never see you on this side of town
cause you never liked exploring with me

I know I'll never bump into you when I book a show
cause every time I asked you'd never go

I know I'll never board the train car you are on
cause I don't know where you're going to or from

I know I'll never, but I wish I did

I wish we stumbled upon each other
in the middle of the street
I wish somehow somewhere, we would meet
cause I've been thinking about what I'd say

I miss you and
I want to
want you still

I ran into your friends on the internet yesterday
they're the only ones I didn't block from your life

I came upon that old song I wrote for you that winter
February will never be the same

I saw you in my dreams doing our same casual things
cause you still live inside my brain on a loop

I thought I passed you by on an off-chance trip
but it was only me with your memory

I know I'll never, but I wish I did

I wish we stumbled upon each other
in the middle of the street
I wish somehow, somewhere we would meet
cause I've been thinking about what I'd say to you

I miss you and
I want to
want you still

I'm at our old train stop right now
visiting the past
wondering how long this will last

cause all I want is you to want to see me again
to reach out and
shout I'm more than your friend

you love me
and you want to
want me still

I know you'll never, but I wish you did

HAPPY HOLIDAYS

I'm starting to get used to moving through this world
alone
it's quieter and louder all at the same time
I can hear the flurry of strangers more clearly
I feel more one with the mass than before

this time it's not a constant drum of wanting for
someone else
I feel okay, comfortable, at ease
this is my world and it's just me

I'm an only of a divorced family
so, truly deeply, it feels like I am alone
sometimes that makes me want to cry
more often these days I've come to embrace it

so what if I'm alone?

I wonder if others feel this way
this deeply

when I sit alone in the park
I browse around for others like me
like I browse for avocados at the store
looking for softness
but not so much softness that I can feel the core

when my parents die
no one else will feel it like I do
is it the same for siblings?
anyone who has at least two?

I've always felt the panic of not being invited,
included or thought of
but lately I feel the deep underpinning of
"I don't want to die alone"

but I also don't want to live alone
is that the same thing?

my friends don't get it.
I don't think any of them do.
I try not to compare but on days like today
a holiday
and I sit alone
I feel it more

I would be lying if I said that's not why I want kids
it's a big part

I want a big family
cause I want to feel a family

I know it makes me sound ungrateful for what I have
and I am
I am grateful

is it so wrong of me
to want to be thought of consistently?

to feel the love of always being a part of the plan
to not always be the one who is leading and planning
and trying to form my chosen family
when they all have their own families

tears well at the edge

and I just now remember what today is
his last day
all those years ago now

today is the day he decided to leave
like a flame at the end of a candle
slightly simmers once it's reached its edge

independence
freedom
I hope that's what you got
you must have felt so alone
I understand and it still makes me sad

I'll remember you always
you'll always be invited to my life
you'll always be my family

you'll never be alone

LUCKY REALITY

I awake from the dream
to find the nightmare of my present
alone with my broken back
to remind me this is my reality now

I feel less broken than two days ago
but a vase with a hole at the bottom
still won't be able to sustain
the flowers it so desperately wants to display
only dust can settle on a vase with no boundaries

I can't tell if this solitude is good for me
is stepping away, hiding in fear
that I might say something wrong again
I'm scared to move
to knock another loved one out of my life

blame follows me like the rumor started in sixth grade
it doesn't matter if anyone else believes it
if I do then I'm doomed

so I blame myself
cause that's easier
than sitting in the fact that I hurt you
when I sit in that
I can feel my blood cells yell in upheaval

they want out
they didn't sign up for this
get to a donation bank as soon as possible
they want another host to welcome them
into a new home

one with family and friends and warmth
one that isn't plagued by a family-haunted
with mental illness
with destructive behaviors
with pain

this haunting is not new to me
two grandfathers forever dead
never to know my face
I'll never know their voice

one grandmother haunting still
in the struggle of her children
each aching to come to terms with a different god

my god didn't help
when I couldn't get out of the numbness
the drugs didn't help either
time lost to time

was I born with this hole then?
have I only now come to see the leak
that's been spilling out this whole time

the joke is I've been filling a cup
that could never be filled
is that it?
is that the punchline I've been missing?

is broken a default
that only a lucky few get to be born into?

lucky to be so aware

lucky to have depths of empathy
born from my generational pain

what an heirloom to inherit
lucky to be alive

so so so
lucky

welcome to my living nightmare
or what some may call
reality

lucky
lucky
reality

STILL AWAKE

I've got a chain chest
weighing me down, full of regrets

This I can't survive
I'm already barely alive

WHERE WERE WE?

my skin is bleeding off
ever since I heard the news yesterday
the smell of you faded
but fresh wounds still form
like you're holding a knife at my door

I don't know what's worse
that you two are together
or that I still want you even with it all
that I'm still willing to give it all away again
for the chance that you'll show up or call

I wrote two letters this morning
one for you and one for her
I want to send them both
but I'll wait a week or more

torturing myself by hoping you'll want me
seeing you everywhere and only wanting to
rush in too
run to you and kiss you
make it all feel better, go away

I want you to know I've changed
and I want to feel you have too
but knowing what I know now
I don't know if you have

I don't know if you will or want to
knowing you are with her
when there's part of you that knows
it will kill me

and it has

the tears won't stop coming
and I can't clear my mind
I'm walking 'til my feet fall off
walking 'til I can make it all rewind

back to when you wanted to move in
and she wanted that too
but I wasn't ready and felt like it wasn't right
even with the love

back to when I stopped showing up for myself
and gave everything to you
I know you didn't ask for that
and it made us break further from truth

back to when everything felt forced
even the hugs we shared felt heavy
to when I wanted to be with you one last time
and one last time was too many

there's not enough steps in the world to
walk me out of love with you
not enough time to pass
to stop the hope of wanting us still

not enough knife wounds or sorries
goodbyes or partings
to make me stop wishing you would show up

I'll die at this coffee shop
with not an ounce of luck

I'll give you my heart and I'll give it again
until I die and I'm left wondering

were we ever even friends?

THIS STILL COMES TO ME,
EVEN AFTER IT ALL

I hope matcha makes you think of me
I hope it brings back that memory
of me telling you I was falling

I hope the winter comes and goes again
and you have found a new friend
that's different from the one I was calling

I hope you come visit the cats
and see the life you could have had
and wish you could redo the past

but most of all
I hope you never move on
cause I'm not sure I can

YOU'LL ALWAYS BE
THE ONE

I feel less alone
when I hear you moan
but it's not a real sound
only my own come down

from our time together
I still question, what was the weather?
these days I can't figure it out
forecasted for progress but I just regress

back into our past, my past
since I don't know what you feel
I can only sense my life peel

away I go
hope you miss me, you probably don't
you probably are playing a game
not of life, but the same

you woke up every morning
and went straight to it
never stopping to be with me
you wanted to escape, now I see

one day I hope I stop beating myself up
stop questioning why my love wasn't enough
stop seeing your faults as my misgivings
start seeing the flaws in your living

but you'll always be my first
and for that you'll always be protected

no matter how often you didn't show up
I'll consider you a golden cup

strong and sturdy
humble and hungry
a collectible item that I'll never fill
lonely on a shelf, I hope

I don't want to collect more of you,
there will always only ever be one
the one who broke me
the one who took more treasures than I won

the one who carries more of me than they'll know
the one who didn't show

the one who said it was too much and left
the one who said I was too much
and they couldn't be next

the one I begged to sleep with me, to rest
the one who never came to bed until I was distressed

the one I love and would love over and over again
the one who could still have me
if they showed up differently,
with more honesty and accountability

the one I will always give a second chance
the one who'll never ask for one

the one who's betrayed me and the memory of us
the one who I don't know anymore
the one I don't know if I can trust

you'll always be the one
the first, I hope of many

I'll always have a place here
in my heart
for you

and when you wake up next to someone new
I hope you have a space for me
whisper my name in your brief insanity

and I hope

they'll ask,
who?

TORN AND WRINKLED

we steam our clothes just to wrinkle them
we wash them just to add more stains
we mess up and mix up and wish that it was us
that had it perfectly together always

I'd rather my clothes stay wrinkled
I rather be covered in stains
I rather be lived in and worn through, torn to pieces
it shows my pain

I wear it like a badge
to prove that I'm living
I proclaim it in spaces of giving
we share and we take but we all feel the same
and I love to release my misgivings

cause I know there are more tears to come
more seams that will split at inopportune moments
fibers will fall, skirts will shred
and I'll still be here after it all

nature or not
I'll be telling my tale
of how largely I lived
that my clothes had to fail

they escaped and disintegrated on the way
but I still stay

I still get up
still try
I still wander

even when I don't know why

I still float
when I feel I'm sinking
I still glide
when all I feel is stuck

I still make up my face up
when I'm fed up of heads-up
something's headed your way
keep up

I have stains to prove
of where I've been bruised
I have wrinkles that cover my resume
they say exactly what they need to say

that I'm loving
I'm trying
I'm sick of buying

everyone else's fantasy
sold to believe in a majesty
but I never signed up to bow down

I lounge in my lived-in
loved for their misgivings
torn exactly
where I need to be
in my wrinkled destiny

WHOLE HOLE

it's hard to live with myself these days
the thud on the door saying

        will you ever be loved again?

I want to crawl back to him
I want his love back
want to come home to someone
who wants to make dinner with me

        as we stare up at the Milky Way I ask
                what love is to them

        as I listen to the trickle of their replies
                the smell of sulfur
           covers every inch of our thighs
              I know I was in love too
        and that it was torn out of me

my thoughts pound like a hard baseline
telling me I should have been better
been more grateful

        a drip of cow shit hits my shoulder

I fucked up
Something's wrong with me
I'm wrong

the inner voice tortures me
until my body is covered in hives
blisters puss out my insecurities

and I think how could he have loved me like this?

could he ever love me again?

the thoughts feel like evidence brought to trial
here lies a woman who relied too much on another
to do what only she could

guilty on all charges

I can only inspire myself to start
I can only support myself to start
I can only be secure in myself to start
I can only love myself to start

I thought I had
I want to believe I did to some extent
but as I unravel more each day
I question reality and I just feel
shame

not enough
too much
my thoughts kill me over and over again
I'm shocked this disease of the mind lasts so long

I've been thinking about all the things I need to do
before I die
because it feels like it's coming soon

I've been hoping you reach out to see me
because I can't live with that goodbye

I've been trying to play good human

because I don't want to die

not yet
not this way
not wishing it would all go away

I'll patch up the hole at the bottom of my cup
the leak that's been letting out my energy
it's projections leaking out the best of me

as the drain shrinks to nothing
my vessel becomes whole again
my drops no longer drip away as fast as they came in

I didn't want to fill that hole
I didn't want to admit that it was there
didn't want to speak the truth I could already feel

my filling was flailing fully failing my feelings
full of nothing, open leaks leaving less and less left
than at the beginning

in the before times
those leaks were of my own doing, in part
the deception thinking
that this train of negative self-talk
would be my motivation, a good start

but putting myself down just puts myself down
and giving you more of me leaves less for me

letting you go helps me patch up the hole
saying goodbye gives growth ground to glow
in my own head

I didn't want to do it before
I didn't want to accept it
but I do want my cup to be full
I want a whole hole

so I patch up the misstep in miss-giving more of
myself mercilessly
so that my cup can fill up again

so I might feel anything but emptiness
so I might hold my vase
and appreciate the wetness it holds
and how its exterior upholds

for me

I'll patch up
to release you

free me

fuller than before
when there was no hole

WHAT IS IT?

as I look back
I wonder

> why the pain inspires
> so much more than the pleasure

is it that I am so much more desperate
for a cure now then I was then

> when I never wanted
> that period to end

is it that I was fully living
fully enveloping myself in

> every moment
> every touch
> every decision

is it that it was pure
the rush of newness, of longing
finally risen to belonging

or is it that it didn't inspire enough?

I scour my notes, my mind, my memories
for the feelings that set it apart

I found a video of my love confession
to no one else but for myself in four years time

on the other side of this descent

I made another video for future me to see
and to comfort her now

I told her she'll be happy again
and she's found something different
something magical
something awe-inspiring
something worth all this pain

somehow

MY CAT PEE

self-hatred suffocates
more than the smell of cat pee
soaking into my mattress

it ties me up with a gag over my mouth
and tells me to sing as loud as I can or it will shoot

it forces me to watch as my father is stabbed in the
heart and survives it
he bleeds out in front of me 'til the very last moment
he can actually survive this torture
but I don't survive

my body becomes a one-night hotel room
discounted rates get bought out
by the next closest trauma

he fills my head and threatens to move in permanently
he doesn't care what state the room is left in
"the maid will clean it up"

but the maid never comes
so the next haunting enters me
and threatens to burn the whole place down

it almost did once
it got so close
there are still permanent burn marks
that cover the walls

I'm not sure how deep the damage goes

part of me doesn't want to take off the wallpaper
to look
cause what if I see worse than I expect
that it threatens to collapse at any moment's notice
to fall and never inhabit again

it feels closer now than it has since
that first fire of 2019
I hate this feeling
and I know hating it only makes it worse

self-hatred loves when I hate it
I overfeed it like a spoiled upper-class kid on
Christmas morning
not a thought in the world but "what did I get?"

my Christmas wasn't like that
I hoped I would get one thing on my list
a 24 set of gel pens
I got an off-brand paint set instead
then I sat through countless friends rattle off
everything they got that year

while I sit in a lower humidity, what's wrong with
me?
why don't I get to have what I want?
self-hatred awakens to give me all the reasons
why I don't deserve what I want

it spins a story better than any HBO special
weaving worries I have into weighted baggage
I still carry
when will the kid get lighter?
when you actually deserve it

it gnaws at my ear and threatens to make it worse
it taunts me and says I'm ungrateful

that I've had it good
it tells me I'm pathetic
and to stop whining, that's why I'll never be happy

not because of him but because of me

when it's done for what feels like weeks
it checks out of the room

leaving a tattered shell
of what used to be my safe place
no one can see the damage that's been done
unless they look close, in my eyes

they threaten to tell the story
I don't want anyone to know
that I've been made to feel like I'm not good enough
like I don't deserve happiness
like I'll never get what I want
that my problems sink in stronger than
the stench of cat pee

MY LONELY COMPANY

I feel the quiet in my temples grow louder
does this mean I'm dead?

I've fantasized about having a real disease
knowing the date it will end so I can plan backwards

I think I'll spend all my money and go into as deep of
debt as humanly possible and then
end it when the flow ends
it won't be unlike where my dad is right now

I also think if I have a doctor's stamp of disaster
maybe people will show up
maybe I'll feel a sense of family and community
surround me
maybe not, maybe I'll feel more alone

though that feels hard to imagine feeling more alone
than I do right now

no calls, no texts, no plans
no "I thought of you today"
I try to send those texts to those I love
hoping one day I'll get one too

you've been on my mind
I'd love to see you
I care about you and have felt your absence

even just a hey, how are you doing

I want to stop waiting around

hoping someone will show up
but my humanity keeps catching up to me
it's forever in a state of remission

it's too bad
I've been diagnosed with living
I'm taking the prognosis harder than I expected

probably because I thought at some point
it has to get better
doesn't it?
isn't that what we're promised?
better, growth, upward motion

I blame myself constantly
I grieve my past optimistic compulsion
I miss her the most

I've steeped in shame longer than I realized
I uncover more of it every day and it scares me

how can anyone undo this level
of pain, hurt, wrongness

how have I carried this for 30 years and still
the diagnosis stays the same
you are here to live

I did get a text today
someone thought of me in their suicidal state

I don't know what that means
I don't know if I can help

I don't know if I can be that close to something I
already know too well

suicide is not a punchline to throw when you mean
you've had a bad day
or your sandwich order is wrong
or you can't afford tickets to see your favorite artist
sing their favorite song

suicide is an unfortunate friend I know well
she's visited me five times
six if we include this text, which I do

suicide is the cancer of sitting with your lived
diagnosis for too long
it offers hope that you don't have to suffer
I wish I could say otherwise but it's true

it's not that, it's not hope
it's an end

and I understand
I understand what living with pain that feels too big
for one lifetime feels like

and how it pulls you down a path of possible
alternatives to the torture of reality

at times
but sometimes those at times
are years
and really how much can one person take?

I wish I had time to talk to each of them

my loved ones who have gone

I wish we could have shared more
I don't know if it would have changed anything
but it would have been nice to know them deeper
in that way

they're not alone
you're not alone
I'm not alone, even though I'm lonely

I guess for now
that will be
what keeps me company

SHRIVELED BROKEN BITS

uncovering the shards that have embedded themselves
into my life
feels like finding out I'm not human
that this world I've known
has never been what I thought

I replace the foreign object with splinters
it's an improvement and still I bleed
the oozing connects me to a handful of others
who aren't in the room

one woman who feels like she started it all
but truly there's no way to know
when the sun first rose and will it ever end?

one friend who is prey
just like I had been at five

carrying this weapon
makes the grim reaper look like
a neighborhood bunny
there's no way to know how many lives he's taken
or how many futures erased

I want to ask you if I hurt you in this way too
but my mouth is sewn to my hand
and my hand is no longer attached to my body

I drip everywhere I walk
dried disappointments shape the path
that one day my daughter will walk
if I don't exorcize this now

so I stab the source
puncture the past, let it live through life now
as long as it needs
'til it passes and I transform

from shriveled broken bits
to something more formed

YOUR GREATEST GIFT

you've given me a great gift
one of the greatest gifts I've ever received

I can only see it now
you leaving was a gift

I don't know if I would have ever been able to let go
to say goodbye

it was hard enough even when you did
hard to let go of you then

now, I've felt the shift my acceptance has brought
that it is what I need and want

even with how hard it's been
and how much I've missed you
and wanted you
and considered trying to get you back

you did what I couldn't
which was leave

say this wouldn't work
we both need something else
and that's okay

I wanted to force us to be what we needed
and wanted for each other

Thank You for seeing that we didn't have to do that
that we didn't have to do that to each other

Thank You for making a hard decision
for being honest
and truthful
even though it hurt

Thank You for doing what I couldn't

I'm so grateful for our chapter
even though
I have never known
deeper pain of heartbreak disaster

and this, you, were the first to show me
show me this level of pain

I'm getting closer to being happy

I can see a far-off distance where we sit together
as friends
still with so much love
and care for each other
but in a different way

seeing that
the potential of it
helps me feel and know happiness will find me again

this lesson of letting go is hard
and has opened my eyes
to how many others I haven't been able to let go of

has opened my mind to
letting go
as an act of love

to know I feel love
so deep
I let them go
in love

I know you really did love me
that you do
even though you are flawed
and made mistakes
just like me

I hurt you
you hurt me

we also helped each other see more of ourselves
get closer to where we are both going

I hope I get to see you sing again
I hope you get to read my book

you helped me
helped give these new gifts to me

your greatest gift is a catalyst
for so many more gifts
I'm just beginning to receive

so Thank You
I will always love you
my friend
my first

I will always love
this greatest gift

LOVING AGAIN

SECRET BEACH

tingling from the intentional
the waves gently touch my toes
you gently ask if I want more

Thank You is all I can muster
Thank You Thank You Thank You

I feel special
feel thought of, considered
I'm not trying and it's freeing to be here
just be pretty

your little book of secrets
are actually thoughtful proses
unfolding each other, who knows this

about you
I feel grateful
happy I stepped out, instead of scurrying away
like I wanted to
when I started this day

I feel calm, at peace
settled in the pace
I'm a slow-burn
and you said great
that's more than okay

relief caresses my body
reminds me I'm in control
I felt your kindness enter my soul

what is your favorite part about me?

your shoulders are amazing

what makes you sing at night?

your eyes tell me everything

what makes you feel alive?

I would feel safe to cry

you love my lips

I like your attention on them, every last bit

Thank you is all I have in my body
I feel okay to move on

happy to be reminded
that I am special
I am worth it
I am thought of

I have been
all along

WHAT'S LEFT
FOR WHAT'S NEXT

it happened
I fell in love again
this time with a book

the rush of wanting
my sleep is totally fucked

every waking minute and hour
all I think about is them
all I want is them
much like how it was with us

it's been a heady mix of
everything
like trying to figure out if your ranch has expired
just with a sniff test

it looks the same, feels the same
and only the sent slightly suspect

the feelings in the depths of my stomach
feel more vibrant
more alive
I question if that's how it started when you first
arrived

I can't tell if the memories have faded
or if they were never there in the first place
I think the first, since your face is now shaded

yet you're here in this newness too

I go back and forth
from seeing and feeling this blast of desire
and then some gentle reminder
of us

can I still call us that?
us

you'll never know this street the way I do
you may never see the cats and how they grew

you say, "that's not how life works"
but do you know all of my quirks?

I finally did what you used to do so perfectly
so exquisitely
by myself this time
revolutionary

you taught me and I learned
that credit you've earned

I Thank You, deeply, truly
I'm so grateful for this magic, it's juicy

not unlike the dimensions we used to visit together
I don't know if they're the same places or untethered

all I know is that I feel myself moving
I never thought it would happen

I touch a new page
and I'm rushed with passion

Thank god!
I needed this

now all that's left for what's next
is a new first kiss

HEY STRANGER HEY

I'm oozing desire down Diversey
if someone stopped me
they'd want me, here, now

I'm sparked with sensual serendipity
waiting to happen

                                    just say the word

my come on
is my presence

                        presently forcing you forward

no one can resist
so it's okay
you feel like this

it's that feeling

                            of finally pleasing yourself
                    and soaking in the erotic efficiency

it's that feeling

                                    of feeling everything
                            full-bodied and bountiful

fuck I'm sexy
I want me
again and again and again

if I could handle my hips

                                            I would

if I could kiss my clit

                                            I would

if I could grind on my groin

                            I wouldn't be writing this
                            I wouldn't need you to join

the after-effects of
this kind of attention is infectious

                            watch out you've already got it

lucky you
savor it
cause soon you'll be touching yourself
remembering this day

when I walked by you
on the street

and hardly said hey

BOAR'S HEAD

standing on water
I see myself more

the soaked mayonnaise in my head
tastes better than I thought

expectations dissolve on my tongue

I've never stood here before
seeing what my future could be
so clearly, in front of me
in the form of a life already lived

Jessica whispers, "I'm so excited for you"
all I can say is Thanks
as the crunch of the jalapeno kettle
settles in my soul

I'm happy
and I'm happy I can sit in it
fully feel it and practice
the embrace of her
my no-pressure, high-achieving cold-cut

it would be different without the mayonnaise
less passive time spent with my partner in our house
more time with new flavors

a new seasoning
we left the cracked black pepper
took the support of the non-default destinations
I'm happy you're here with me

the access in excess
no negative limit
abundant with alignment

Thank You, friend,
Thank You, you
Thank You, mayonnaise

LOVE IS

Love you have me

I feel you like the hot wax that dripped on my finger
quickly solidified
stuck on as if it's part of me

you sink in
like the coconut oil I slather
in every crevice of my cracked soul

I'm still excavating deeper
to find more comfort
more of myself
more of you, Love

my knees can feel the rain
before my skin does
they tell me to take a minute
in those moments

when I feel the rush of hate
of betrayals marinated
a hard crust has formed

I shelter the part of me
I need the most

Love, don't be scared
I know it's suffocating
to feel the density of destiny

no control
no say
no choice in whether to walk away

foolish me, to think you left
or that I lost you in that phase
it's still you, just with a new eyeliner on your face

you're there in the heat of my heart
you are the stir of fury
you care, we've never been apart

Love, I now know you'll never go away
at one point that scared me,
more than you leaving
I didn't think I could be with you,
without being with him

Love, I know that's not what I want
to have built and built to this beautiful sphere
of energy
of magic
you don't just burst, you brighten

I won't always have you

I'll always be with you

                    you'll always be with me

a different state
of time
of mind
unwind

we won't be tangled in each other
blended as one

I won't caress your neck hair
                              you won't watch me run

I won't listen to the clicks
from your hands in the distance

                    you won't hear about my next
                 and what the doctor said is different

I won't call
                                   you won't text

I won't know

                              you won't hear

and still,
Love will
Love has
Love is

Love is

You
                 And
                                        Me

                 Separately

IN HOPES WITH HOPE

my soul thaws in the sun
melting away the pounce of "you need to change"
"you're the problem"
"what's wrong with you?"

revealing my true self
the self that loves who I am
the self that's always lept into the path past fear
always taken the way that wasn't there
in Hopes
with Hope

the hard exterior of settle to have something
the helmet that's held my pain and screamed
this is not worth it
hideaway
cracks have started to form
Thank god

I'm so ready for the requiem
ready to bask in the sun that's peaking its head
but that I couldn't feel
until now

Thank You god for the sun
Thank You god
that I can feel something on my skin again
Thank god I can Thank god again

if last night's version of me could only feel this now

I held her, that's the best I could do

as she wept every last piece of her soul out
spilled on the floor
wrapped in a blanket of I give up
and it was exactly what I needed
to crack
again

I used to hate Hope
curse her and wish she never cursed me constantly

Hope for a better life
Hope for a partner who was my partner
Hope for love who loves me back
Hope for a friend who can forgive me
Hope for moving past fear
for taking the leap
the risk
and finally
finally
finally
finally
finally

basking in the sun of "it was all worth it"

Hope lives deep in my bones
deeper than the fear,
insecurities,
or "why mes"

Hope moves my muscles
it's the only reason I'm still here
this bitch
my bitch

Hope

we're not fully friends
again
I can't fully feel her
yet

but the crack in the armor is the start
for the next phase

to love
again

in Hopes with Hope

TIE-DYE GIRL

Tie-dyed but not tied down
how you sparkle and glow with the wind

you're lighter than a feather
you keep teaching it how to relax and where to begin
your smile radiates like the rays of the sun

sunshine, be mine
although I know I can't own you or prone you
I don't want to
you're free, you always will be

your gentle tenderness knows no bounds
it softens and molds
even when you can sense others' frowns
your joy is never ending
like a stream with no final destination

I love you my little one
I feel you here, how
your laughter and light make it easier now

easier to love
to listen
to hold
and glisten

you make it easy to hold others
tell them it will be okay
your trust is disarming, your magnetism alarming,
it knocks all doubts and judgment away
you simply breathe and play!

sometimes I hold you and try to let you live again
sometimes I remind myself you're more than
just my friend

sometimes, when I need it, I tell you I'm scared
and sometimes you hold me
and tell me that you'll always be there

I love you little one
you inspire me to grow
you remind me of the roots inside me
and how lovely it is to know

you are a sun to many
and a lover to some
you are a star in this world
and I'm so happy that you've come

let your colors melt into patterns of freedom
let the swirls spin solace to those who need them
let the tie-dye you love never leave your soul

and let your love shine always
you are magical whole

Love never leaves you

she finds a new way to live
again & again

MANTRAS

Mantras have been a lifeline in my healing journey, offering comfort and peace when I struggled to find it elsewhere. Here are some that have profoundly shaped my path forward. I hope they bring you support and inspiration on your journey.

It's safe to put this down right now.

Stillness is nurturing.

Acceptance is welcome.

Trust the process.

Be gentle.

There is no rush.

Let the softness flow over.

Peace is here.

Your light radiates.

You and your material are enough.

You are enough.

You are not alone.

You are worthy.

You are safe.

You are abundant.

You are awesome, just as you are.

You are healing.

You are human, it's ok to make mistakes.

You are exactly where you need to be.

You are exactly where you are meant to be.

I trust you.

I believe in you.

I support you.

I am here for you.

I know it's hard right now.

I got you.

I hear you.

I am listening.

I am so proud of you.

I love you.

ACKNOWLEDGMENTS

Thank you to my mom, Kathy Pedigo, and dad, Mark Pedigo. You have always taught me to be friends with my emotions and to give them space to live. I will always be grateful for your encouragement and support!

Tim Pedigo, Karen Pedigo, Ann, Bill, Nyla Anderson, Garrison Anderson, Sarah Anderson, David Pedigo, Johnathan Pedigo, Alexa Tecarro, and Greyson Cox. Thank you for showing me what family can be. Thank you for listening and lifting me at every step of the way. It fills my heart when we fill a home together, thank you for your love and light.

To my chosen family, Mackenzie Kramer, Sophie, Samantha Morrow, and Simedar Jackson. You have held me and helped me at every turn of life. Thank you for your love, friendship, and community. Thank you for sharing your life with me and embracing me when I've shared mine. I am so grateful to have you all as sisters.

Thank you Lauryn, Eliza Uptown-Green, Eric Lopez, Rebecca D, Shelby Deutsch, Elaine Golden, Rogue, Kailyn Bear, Rubi, Monica Couvillion, Emiley, Marina Mitas, Kay Nieckarz, Hayley Vaughn, Piere Trent, Scott Campbell, and Jeff Menezes. Thank you for coming over with flowers and food, talking for hours on the phone, making me laugh again when I never thought I would, walking with me in silence, and just being there. Thank you forever for making me feel less alone.

Thank you to my therapist Alex, I am so grateful for your guidance in my unfolding. Thank you for holding me and opening a safe space to dive deeper into my pain.

Rumi Tsuchihashi, Cathy Bissegger, Dave Lewis, Simone Hall, Kathryn Proffitt, Beth Cole, Tim Smith, and Sarah Lacy for your mentorship, companionship, support, and encouraging words. You are all my role models, thank you for showing me what is possible and helping me make it possible every single day.

Sagwa and Simbah, your companionship has changed my life for the better. It has been such a joy to raise you two fur babies. Thank you for all you teach me every single day. You have brought so much joy and softness to my life. Thank you for cuddling and following me around, you are the best and I will never stop telling you that.

Thank you to my First Love, without you, I would not know love in the way I do now. Thank you for sharing your life with me during the time we had together. This book would not exist without you, I am forever grateful for your love. You have opened up my life, my heart, and left me forever changed. You will always hold a beautiful place in my heart, I love you.

There are so many others who have influenced these pages, helped me, and who live on the pages of this book. Thank you for your role in my life. I hope peace has found you. I pray that healing and love surround you each and every day.

I have been in and felt so much movement this past year in writing, gathering, and creating this book. With that movement, I am so grateful for the amount of physical movement I've been privileged to do. Each and every one of the places I've visited this year helped me move through a different stage of my processing. These places have helped me unravel and re-ravel. I am so grateful for their nurturing grounds and the spirits that guided me there. Their influences grace these pages. Here are the places I visited this year, in the order I went to them:

Chicago, Illinois
Mexico City, Mexico
Zipolite, Mexico
Brooklyn, New York
Hampton Bays, New York
Kettle Moraine State Forest, Wisconsin
Yosemite National Park, California
Mammoth Lake, California
San Francisco, California
Point Beach State Forest, Wisconsin
Delhi, New York
Honolulu, Hawaii
Kailua-Kona, Hawaii

To my angels — Nathan Pedigo, Elaine Sorber, Elden Holldorf, and Mary Clark. Thank you for all the moments you still visit me, reminding me why I'm here. I miss you always.

With all my heart
over & over
again & again,

Renee

If you or someone you know struggles with mental health, here are a list of some resources:

Al-Anon, for families and friends of alcoholics
anon.org

Alcoholics Anonymous (AA)
aa.org

BIPOC Support
callblackline.com
(800) 604-5841

National Alliance on Mental Illness
nami.org

National Suicide Prevention Hotline
988lifeline.org

Peer Support Warmline (National)
wildfloweralliance.org
(888) 407-4515

Peer-led Virtual Mental Health Support
peersupportspace.org/daily-gatherings

Suicide & Crisis Hotline
Call or text 988

Trans Support
translifeline.org
(877) 565-8860

ABOUT THE AUTHOR

Renee Pedigo, a native of Oak Park, IL, began her creative journey as a fashion designer in New York City. With a lifelong passion for performing and writing, she initially embraced these outlets as forms of personal therapy before choosing comedy as a creative medium. Starting in stand-up, Renee soon expanded to sketch and improvisation, performing at renowned venues like The Second City and The Upright Citizens Brigade. Her work is known for its unique blend of humor and authenticity, always infused with reliably raw vulnerability.

These days, Renee teaches improv classes in Chicago while continuing to explore and refine her diverse creative pursuits. Her evolving projects span producing, screenwriting, and songwriting. You can catch her work online and at local Chicago theaters.

This is Renee's debut published collection of poetry and musings. Follow her on social media to stay updated on her latest creative endeavors.